DON'T LEAVE!!!!!!

Codependency and Attachment

Mary Crocker Cook, D.Min., LMFT, LAADC, CADCII

Don't Leave!!!!

© 2014 Mary Crocker Cook

ISBN: 978-1-61170-187-6

Printed in the USA and UK on acid-free paper.

 Robertson Publishing™
www.RobertsonPublishing.com

To purchase additional copies of this book go to:
amazon.com
barnesandnoble.com

Don't Leave!!!! Codependency and Attachment was written as a "lay-person" version of *Awakening Hope. A Developmental, Behavioral, Biological Approach to Codependence.* Awakening Hope is used as a textbook in Alcohol and Drug programs in the United States. This is the "fun" version, and I hope you enjoy reading it as much as I enjoyed writing it.

I just picked up my 25 year chip. I got sober in Al-anon - I stayed sober in Al-anon. And every time I have seriously thought about drinking, felt overwhelmed by a desire to drink, it's been triggered by a relationship issue.

Every time. No exceptions.

The picture on the next page represents my Codependency bottom:

First there was me

Then there was Him

Then there was only Him

Then He left

Then there was no one

At its heart, Codependency is a set of behaviors developed to manage the anxiety that comes when our primary attachments are formed with people who are inconsistent or unavailable in their response to us.

Our anxiety-based responses to life can include over-reactivity, image management, unrealistic beliefs about our limits, and attempts to control the reality of others to the point where we lose our boundaries, self-esteem, and even our own reality.

Ultimately, Codependency is a chronic stress disease, which can devastate our immune system and lead to systemic and even life-threatening illness.

Afraid the pain will kill me

Afraid it won't

And I'll be left

On the wrong side of the dirt

Why Does Attachment Matter?

Secure bonding and attachment between caregivers and their children sets the foundation for our future connections with others.

Bonding generally refers to the parents' emotional investment in their child, which builds and grows with repeated meaningful shared experiences.

Attachment usually refers to the tie between the infant and parents, which the child actively initiates and participates in.

The quality of attachment largely determines our developing
sense of self and approach to the world around us.

Placement in the foster care
system

Serious mental illness creating
emotional and mental
unavailability

Abusive relationships that absorbs
the majority of the caretaker's
energy

Incarceration

Deployment

Alcohol/Drug addiction

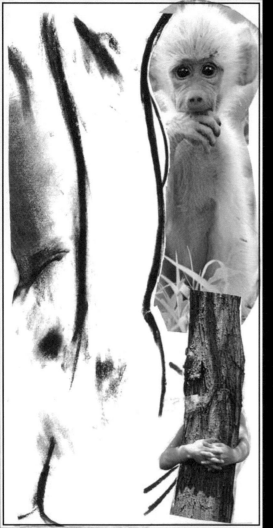

Unspoken Void

Groundless

Holding on for life

Seems the right thing to do

But I forget why

None of these reasons have anything to do with LOVE for the child.

However, we cannot possibly know this, believing that the unavailable parent is not available due to some defect within us. We believe that if we were "enough" the parent would CHOOSE to be available.

This begins the "going to the hardware store to get milk" pattern we talk about in Al-Anon

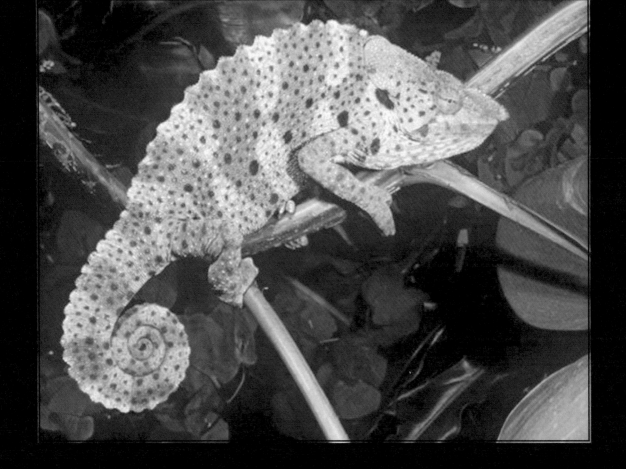

As an Anxious Codependent . . .

I need to be aware of you and *your attachment to me* all the time. I can feel it when you're not emotionally or physically available, and get anxious when you feel "distant." I get into action to fix or remove whatever is distracting you from your connection to me.

As an Avoidant Codependent. . .

I learned early in life that crying or asking for attention is pointless. So, I handle my own business, and have almost no expectation that others will meet my needs. I worry about being a burden and looking "needy."

How Does This Look
In Adulthood?

Anxious situations trigger a desire to reach out to a Secure Base in adulthood. People engage in three main strategies to reduce anxiety:

Secure

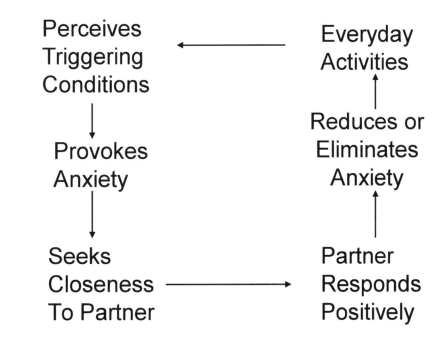

Perceives Triggering Conditions → Provokes Anxiety → Seeks Closeness To Partner → Partner Responds Positively → Reduces or Eliminates Anxiety → Everyday Activities → Perceives Triggering Conditions

What does this look like?

When we have a stressful day we can share it with someone we trust to hear and see us ACCURATELY, and someone who will provide us support. As a result, our anxiety drops and we can return to our lives.

Avoidant

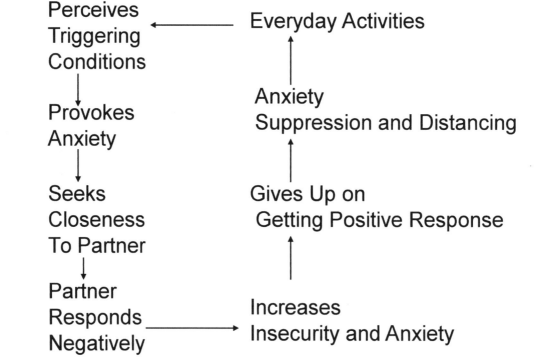

Perceives Triggering Conditions ← Everyday Activities

Perceives Triggering Conditions → Provokes Anxiety

Provokes Anxiety → Seeks Closeness To Partner

Seeks Closeness To Partner → Partner Responds Negatively

Partner Responds Negatively → Increases Insecurity and Anxiety

Increases Insecurity and Anxiety → Gives Up on Getting Positive Response

Gives Up on Getting Positive Response → Anxiety Suppression and Distancing

Anxiety Suppression and Distancing → Everyday Activities

What does this look like?

We have a stressful experience and reach out to someone who cannot see and hear us ACCURATELY. So they respond negatively, maybe push us away or give us advice. We give up, squish down our anxiety, and go back to our lives. And handle it ourselves. After a while we may even forget it.

Anxious

Perceives Triggering Conditions ←——— Everyday Activities

↓

Provokes Anxiety

↓

Seeks Closeness to Partner ←————————

↓

Partner Responds Negatively ——————→ Increases Insecurity And Anxiety

What does this look like?

When a stressful situation comes up we reach out to someone who i not available emotionally. Maybe they are worried about something else, or maybe they're loaded. But instead of going on with our lives we keep trying to get them to respond to us. We keep talking and talking . . . we are more worried now that they aren't listening than we were about the original situation!

Submerged

Gasping for air

A vague memory

Of me

Before

This is the
foundation
for adult
Codependency

How Does Anxious and Avoidant Codependency Show up in Our Behavior?

Lack Of Attunement

I am so aware of what other people need and how connected or disconnected they are from me that I pay no attention to my own internal needs and wants. I don't know if I'm tired, don't know what I'm feeling, may not even know what I look like.

Lack of Attunement
with Others

Because I don't read my own internal signals well, I have difficulty accurately reading how I affect other people. I don't always recognize when I'm intrusive or in other people's space because my INTENTION is to help. No one taught me to pay attention to feelings — so I don't know how to accurately interpret it when either one of us has a feeling!

Distrusting the Attachment of Others
to the Codependent

I am never sure that a relationship is solid- I can't trust that you love me even when you say you do because I KNOW this could change. I'm always looking for the warning signs that you're changing your mind and so find ways to try and EARN your love.

Escalation to
Protect Attachment

I'll create scenes and drama to get you to takes me seriously and stay attached to me.

When I feel you're distant, I'll stir up something to get you to pay attention to me so I can feel that we're connected again. Maybe I'll accuse you of cheating or break into your email account. A moderate response never feels like it's ENOUGH!

Denial of Dependency
or Attachment Needs

Because I always have a plan "B", waiting for you to leave, I don't let myself feel fully invested or attached to you. In fact, I tell myself that I don't "need" that kind of connection with someone and people who do are "weak." When you eventually leave because I gave you the impression you didn't matter that much to me, I'll say, "See, I told you so."

Avoiding Intimacy

I want you to be intimate with me so I can see what you're thinking and feeling to better monitor how you feel about me. But I don't want to share what's going on with me, even if I know because it would make me vulnerable and I might start to depend on you for support – then lose you. This feels like too great a risk to take.

Walls Instead of Boundaries

I have all kinds of walls between us. Maybe it's silence, being hysterical and over-reacting, staying drunk, being passive, always angry, or playing stupid so you will make all the decisions and take all the responsibility.

Whatever I'm doing, it makes me hard to get to know.

There

I'm still in there

Ridiculous

Awake

Codependency Can Make Us Physically Ill – It Can Kill Us

Physiology of the Stress Response Connected to Codependency

While attachment issues set the emotional and developmental stage for future behaviors, the fight, flight, or freeze response is the physical mechanism that leads to our physical deterioration and lowered immune system. The fight, flight, or freeze response is designed to prepare us to respond to an emergency, not to be a lifestyle!

The Alarm Reaction

When I feel my partner distancing from me, unavailable, or non-responsive I feel:

- Racing heart

- Sweaty Palms

- Nausea

- Impending harm

HYPERVIGILANCE tunes out all information except immediate threat.

Dissociation (Freeze)

If my anxiety becomes too intense, I will "leave my body" so my adrenal system will calm down. I might dissociate which could look like:

1. a distorted sense of time or

2. a detached feeling that you are observing something happen to you as if it is unreal — the sense that you may be watching a movie of your life.

Today we know the body can't tell the difference between an emotional emergency and physical danger. When triggered, it will respond to either situation by pumping out stress chemicals designed to impel someone to flee to safety or stand and fight.

The only way out for a child is for a caring person to hold, reassure, and stabilize them which can happen if a **secure attachment** with the caregiver exists. When primary caregivers are not available to soothe and reassure us, we are left to live through this fight, flight, or freeze system without support. This makes us vulnerable to using alcohol and drugs to calm ourselves down as we get older.

Adrenaline is by far the most important single hormone in regards to stress - taking a major role in the stress reaction, **and stays longer in the body even after our system has settled down again.**

The Destructive Effect of
High Cortisol Levels

What is cortisol? In its normal function, cortisol helps us meet these challenges by converting proteins into energy, releasing glycogen, and counteracting inflammation. For a short time, that's okay. But at sustained high levels, cortisol gradually tears your body down.

Sustained High Cortisol Levels:

- destroy healthy muscle and bone

- slow down healing and normal cell regeneration

- co-opt biochemicals needed to make other vital hormones

- impair digestion, metabolism and mental function

- interfere with healthy endocrine function; and

- weaken your immune system.

The world

Ancient

Mysterious

Undiscovered and uncharted

Mine

So Now What?

I want to remind you that Codependency and attachment issues are not gender based. In fact all of the research points to no difference in attachment styles between men and women.

But healing will not be linear – meaning $a + b + c = d$

You will be addressing issues simultaneously, more like a spiral than a straight line upward.

Anxious or Avoidant Attachment history

Gender and cultural role beliefs

Anxious or Avoidant behavior patterns

Inhabiting your body

- **Support** –

  In recovery we say at least 3 people is a support group.

- **Cognitive Life Raft** –

  Learning about Codependency and Attachment can help you understand what's going on with you.

- **Take an Intimacy Questionnaire** –

  It helps you get a bead on where you are right now.

Bowing in gratitude

Recipient of grace

Saved by a love

Older than time

Inhabiting Your Own Body

Figure out ways to stay conscious of your body — knowing when you're hungry and tired, or need physical movement. Maybe you need to see a doctor and take care of unaddressed health issues.

Develop an
Emotional Vocabulary

You will need to read about emotions, maybe even get a "feeling faces" poster online so you can learn to connect your feelings with labels. This is important because it increases your ability to communicate using your words instead of acting out.

Identify Your
"Little and Unimportant Hurts"

We have unaddressed injuries, broken attachments, and losses that we need to recognize and release. Your experience DOES matter.

Listen To Your Thoughts and Daydreams. We need to pay attention to our inner voice, our inner direction. This may mean journaling or meditating – taking time to listen to yourself without distraction. Treat yourself as though you matter.

Emotional Regulation Tools

Create an emotional regulation tool box. You can gather together scented candles or incense, a favorite blanket, favorite music or sounds, favorite pictures, books on tape, comforting foods ... sensory support to help you bring your system down when you have been triggered.

Are You Using Sex To Release Your Emotions?

Pay attention to ways you use your sexuality. Are you being sexual hoping to feel connected to someone unavailable? This may leave you even lonelier.

Notice Eating, Drinking, Exercising or Any Type of Compulsive or Excessive Behavior. Pay attention to what you are putting into your body or the way you're treating yourself to avoid feeling. It's hard to stay in your feelings, but they WILL pass.

What You Say and Do
Needs to Sync With What You Feel

Pay attention to your gut reactions when you are participating with others. The goal is to be congruent – my insides match my outsides.

Release emotions and resentment. It's important that you share what is happening inside of you rather than ignore it, or it can make you sick. Take the risk to be honest with people – it can be fun!

Physical Touch
and Oxytocin

Oxytocin is a hormone that helps relax and reduce blood pressure and cortisol levels. It increases pain thresholds, has anti-anxiety effects, and stimulates various types of positive social interaction. In addition, it promotes growth and healing.

Finally, you need hugs, time with people who love you, and laughter to increase your oxytocin.

Ancient wisdom

Sifted through the ashes

Not forgotten

Ever present

The Experiences in Close Relationships-Revised (ECR-R) Questionnaire; Fraley, Waller, and Brennan (2000)

The statements below concern how you feel in emotionally intimate relationships. Answer the questions in terms of how you *generally* experience relationships, not just in what is happening in a current relationship. Respond to each statement by giving a number from 1 through 7 to indicate how much you agree or disagree with the statement. 1 = strongly disagree and 7 = strongly agree. At the end of the survey, you will find scoring instructions. Trust me. You can get through this. Use a calculator. Or, again, you can bag scoring the test at all!

1. strongly disagree
2. disagree
3. disagree somewhat
4. neutral
5. agree somewhat
6. agree
7. strongly agree

1. It's not difficult for me to get close to my partner.

2. I often worry that my partner will not want to stay with me.

3. I often worry that my partner doesn't really love me.

4. It helps to turn to my romantic partner in times of need.

5. I often wish that my partner's feelings for me were as strong as my feelings for him or her.

6. I worry a lot about my relationships.

7. I feel comfortable depending on romantic partners.

8. When I show my feelings for romantic partners, I'm afraid they will not feel the same about me.

9. I rarely worry about my partner leaving me.

10. My partner only seems to notice me when I'm angry.

11. I feel comfortable depending on romantic partners.

12. I do not often worry about being abandoned.

13. My romantic partner makes me doubt myself.

14. I find that my partner(s) don't want to get as close as I would like.

15. I'm afraid that I will lose my partner's love.

16. My desire to be very close sometimes scares people away.

17. I worry that I won't measure up to other people.

18. I find it easy to depend on romantic partners.

19. I prefer not to show a partner how I feel deep down.

20. I feel comfortable sharing my private thoughts and feelings with my partner.

21. I worry that romantic partners won't care about me as much as I care about them.

22. I find it difficult to allow myself to depend on romantic partners.

23. I'm afraid that once a romantic partner gets to know me, he or she won't like who I really am.

24. I am very comfortable being close to romantic partners.

25. I don't feel comfortable opening up to romantic partners.

26. I prefer not to be too close to romantic partners.

27. I get uncomfortable when a romantic partner wants to be very close.

28. I find it relatively easy to get close to my partner.

29. I usually discuss my problems and concerns with my partner.

30. I tell my partner just about everything.

31. Sometimes romantic partners change their feelings about me for no apparent reason.

32. When my partner is out of sight, I worry that he or she might become interested in someone else.

33. I am nervous when partners get too close to me.

34. It's easy for me to be affectionate with my partner.

35. It makes me mad that I don't get the affection and support I need from my partner.

36. My partner really understands me and my needs.

Scoring:

1. Some answers need to be reverse scored like this: 1=7, 2=6, 3=5, 4=4, 5=3, 6=2, 7=1. Take all the numerical answers to the following questions and give them a new, reversed score: 1, 4, 7, 9, 11, 12, 18, 20, 24, 28, 29, 30, 34, 36.

2. Take the scores to all the following question numbers and average them. These are the questions you should average: 2, 3, 5, 6, 8, 9, 10, 12, 13, 14, 15, 16, 17, 21, 23, 31, 32, 35. In case you're rusty on third grade math, that means add them all together and divide by the number of answers, in this case, 18. This is your score for attachment-related anxiety. It can range from 1 through 7. The higher the number, the more anxious you are about relationships.

3. Take the scores to the following questions and average them: 1, 4, 7, 11, 18, 19, 20, 22, 24, 25, 26, 27, 28, 29, 30, 33, 34, 36). This score indicates you attachment related avoidance. The higher the score, the more you avoid intimacy in relationships.

Again, many of us score in both ranges, swinging from one level of connection to the other over time. The key is that in both cases, we do not trust that the attachment is secure.

CPSIA information can be obtained at www.ICGtesting.com
Printed in the USA
LVIW01n2252240417
532061LV00002B/18